OFFI

DEVEL

for Professionals

PRESENTATION

SUCCESS

INCLUDING

HOLLYWOOD

Presentation

Secrets

Walter Timoshenko

Edited by Alexandra Timoshenko

Aster House Press

New York
United States of America

PRESENTATION SUCCESS: Official Business Development Series
for Professionals: Including Hollywood Presentation Secrets

ISBN-13: 978-1503119215
ISBN-10: 1503119211

Table of Contents

There are no rules in filmmaking. Only sins. And the
cardinal sin is dullness.

Frank Capra

Introduction to *Presentation Success: Including Hollywood Presentation Secrets*

As Frank Capra noted above, possibly the worst sin you can commit when crafting your presentation is to be boring, lifeless, and dull. We've all sat through *those* presentations. Few of us will remember much more than arriving for the presentation and then leaving, unless someone actually drifted off and snored loudly, or slumped over... The actual heart of the presentation, the exact part that was supposed to move us to action, was soggy and bland, and slipped away forgotten.

Hollywood has it down to a formula. Even though only a handful of movies make it to the very top annually, the techniques and tricks employed in most good films are all aimed at connecting with the audience in multiple ways. Without that connection to viewers, studio execs know that they have no hope of turning a profit. And you don't make connections by being wishy-washy and boring.

How did it make you feel?

Some years ago, I was invited to Al Pacino's Manhattan production company to screen a movie that he was in the process of editing. Instead of theatre seats, we sat in plush recliners to watch the film. After it was over, Al Pacino asked me a question that was an insight into Hollywood success. He didn't wonder, *so how was it?* or *how did you like it?* or *what did you think?* Nope. Instead, he looked me in the eye and asked, "How did it make you *feel?*"

His interest was in "connection" – he wanted to know if his film had *connected* with me emotionally. An audience that "feels" something is engaged, and *that* is very good.

Creating connections

Similarly, when you as a professional create and make presentations, avoiding dullness lets you connect better and move forward faster with your audience. Important, since an audience that doesn't care about your message or your presentation, isn't likely to act.

No connection, no interest, no moving forward.

Taking Hollywood's lead, some of the ways professionals should seek to connect with their audiences include:

- emotionally (relating relevant, touching stories and experiences; discussing common frames of reference such as schools, clubs, and hobbies; expressing passion for your work and services; showing compassion and empathy for others; making them feel your commitment)
- physically (maintaining good eye contact; smiling as appropriate; greeting and exiting with a good handshake; staying out of personal spaces)
- psychologically (thinking in audience-centric terms: *what's in it for them*; using questions to lead conversations rather than trying to force the issue;

demonstrating abilities through case studies and practical examples rather than boasting; using the power of third party endorsements)

- verbally (speaking clearly; not being monotone by maintaining a varied pattern; avoiding industry jargon and obscenity; not speaking over others; not speaking too much; making sure you are being heard)

When done properly, your efforts to *connect*, on any or all levels, should result in a stronger *bond* between you and your audience.

Yet that's not always enough.

Being memorable

We've all met people that we clicked with. However, if later on you don't remember them, or they don't remember you, or both, then what have you gained?

So, you also need to be *remembered*. And to be remembered, you need to be *memorable*. Oh, and just to clarify – the goal is to be *memorable* for the right reasons. No lamp shades. No outrageous behavior.

Following up

Finally, both parties must *follow-up* and actually do something in order to move forward.

Accordingly, while we embark on our journey as professionals, to see what Hollywood techniques we can copy and incorporate into our presentations, let's keep in mind our goals…. to *connect*, to be *memorable*, and to *follow-up*…as a way to stack the odds in our favor for getting maximum potential out of each and every one of our presentations.

Create your own brand and approach

In order to develop a style and approach for making
presentations that will serve you well, we will be looking at what
has worked for the world-dominating master presenters in
Hollywood.

Before we begin, let us agree that nothing is written in stone, and
that your current firm may strongly influence just how much, or
how little, creativity you can inject into your presentations.

At larger firms, you may have less flexibility when it comes to
style and content. "It" is already prepared in a standardized
format that serves your brand. Maybe an entire department
handles the bulk of the writing and packaging. Great, then
operate within that framework and look to put your personal
mark on presentations using some of the ideas we will discuss.

If you are at a smaller firm, or maybe even flying solo, where
you are doing the bulk of the heavy lifting, then you can take the
opportunity to create your own unique approach to making
presentations from the ground up, setting yourself apart from
day one.

Whatever your situation, there is always some degree to which
you can personalize a presentation.

Presentations shouldn't be second-class citizens

It is remarkable how little attention most professionals pay to their presentations – and it shows. Often, final prep is done the night before, or worse yet, on the ride to the prospect's office. There is little, if any, real brainstorming or rehearsal, and their strategy might as well be defined as "a plan to show up at the right address."

I've heard it all: that there is limited time to prepare, that professionals know what to say, that conflicting schedules make it hard to get everyone together to prep, that billable time trumps prep time every time, et cetera. I get it. Still, careful investment of your time into creating memorable presentations has the *very real potential* of paying off exponentially.

Ask those professionals you know who landed large clients. They don't discount their winning presentations, do they? Of course not. In this context, time spent preparing presentations is no less valuable than pure billable time. The only nagging difference that critics will harp on is the fact that billable time generally will be at least 70-80% collectable. On the other hand, "presentation preparing time" has the potential to bring in cash, but could potentially be 100% lost if you're not chosen. Then again, without new business, where would new billable time come from? Half full, half empty glasses…

What works for you?

My own background in what I call *strategic messaging* for brands began on Madison Avenue at Grey Advertising's LHSB. As many ad agency execs were prone to do, we often thought in ":30 second" and ":60 second" increments. Conversely, our endless new business pitches could go on for hours. Nevertheless, whatever we did, we made it our own.

Whether lengthy or brief, our messaging was targeted, concise, and usually very entertaining. We weren't quite "madmen," but we had loads of fun being creative as we got our messages across in memorable ways.

Our chosen "persona" was to be professional but irreverent, edgy yet graceful, and above all, to be overwhelmingly street smart yet generous on behalf of our clients. For decades, these dichotomies worked very well for us. Most of all, we were … *memorable!*

The blandness surrounding you yields opportunities

Today's fast-paced world is truly mind blurring. Mountains of information and messages surround and engulf us. At one end of the spectrum, breaking through the clutter, savvy promoters are endlessly fine-tuning the quantity and quality of their tactics. They are combining traditional mediums with cutting edge social media platforms, adding animation and text to video, complete with sound bites and thematic elements, all the while looking to build trust as much as to entertain.

Professional services messaging usually falls on the other end of the spectrum and is anything but entertaining. Take technicians and statisticians, mix in communications majors with no real financial and client-side experience, and you get a very boring stew. Or, worse yet, the communications majors try to inject some "life" into the mix only to end up with goofy and disjointed messaging. And, it doesn't help that the information that professional services firms need to convey can be rather bland.

I can clearly hear the purists rushing to defend their sacred spreadsheets and voluminous briefs as I type these words. Fine, you got me – the subject matter is often tedious and even mind numbing. But that doesn't excuse presenting it in a similarly dull or inane way.

Herein lies your opportunity.

There are very few professionals out there doing anything remotely close to a "production." Most follow the standard off the shelf approach, and drone on and on. This bland landscape makes it rather easy for you to distinguish yourself with a little smart planning and effort.

Seriously – think about your competitors. Do a little competitive reconnaissance. Does anyone stand out? If not, *why*? Is anyone doing *it* right? If so, why?

At this point, you should be getting a bit excited about the possibilities.

As we delve into the opportunities and possibilities, think in terms of what you can do to incorporate what you learn to stand out.

Connect. Be memorable. Follow-up. Repeat!

---

*People have forgotten how to tell a story. Stories
don't have a middle or an end any more. They
usually have a beginning that never stops beginning.*

Steven Spielberg

A Tale of Two Presentations

***Warning: Rated "R" for Graphic Losses in excess of
one million dollars. Reader Discretion is advised.***

If you don't think honing your presentation skills and
strategically working on the presentations themselves is worth
your while, then maybe we should start with a heartwarming
story of a seven-figure loss.

Act One

Not too long ago, I was sitting through a presentation that was
given by two highly skilled and respected professionals.

Enter the famous stars

One was a CPA of immense talent. The other was an attorney
with a track record of success. They had teamed up in an attempt
to win a large and complex piece of lucrative new business in
which each would play a pivotal role. Truthfully, it was the
ultimate dream team.

The prospective clients and I were personally familiar with each
of them, and we thought that they were eminently qualified. It

was a slam-dunk. Everyone knew it. We were just going through the formalities.

Within a short hour, both professionals would be left to wonder just how they had let such an immense lead slip through their fingers.

The Setting

The presentation was held in a state of the art boardroom high above New York City. As a native of Manhattan, I am rather jaded on cityscapes and vistas. However, even I would agree that this view of the City was spectacular. You could see part of the Hudson and a dozen other iconic landmarks and structures. Yet this view would in no way interfere with the presentation, since remotely controlled shades lowered moments before start time to ensure audience concentration. The room had all the latest electronic conveniences. Screens came out of the ceilings, electrical receptacles were hidden in table legs, chairs barely whispered as they rolled about and reclined, and strong Wi-Fi energy fields flowed through our pores. Barely perceptible microphones in the ceiling seemed to amplify everyone's voices just enough so that you could hear conversations without straining. Almost James Bond-ish.

The Players

There were about a dozen people in the room that day: the two famous professionals, a woman from one of their respective marketing departments who seemed to be in charge of their presentation slides and handouts, and the rest of us who were connected to the prospective client and were there to weigh in on the presentation.

The pre-roll

The meeting had been scheduled for 11:00 AM and the presenters and their marketing person arrived a few minutes early. The marketing person proceeded to place printed copies of a presentation on the boardroom table. She scooped up a pile of plastic imprinted pens from a bag and let them pour out onto the center of the table creating a plastic-pen-edifice. Then she started attempting to connect her computer via Wi-Fi to the boardroom system. IT had to be called to provide passwords and fine-tune the connection. No, it wasn't smooth or classy. Yes, it took several painful minutes. But that was the *least* of the problems that day.

Quiet on the set. Rolling...

After the obligatory introductions, the actual presentation started. Unfortunately, the introductions had been lackluster to say the least. The two professionals had lost the opportunity to capture everybody's attention from the outset. Worse, as they each droned on and on about qualifications, firm rankings, firm history, personal accomplishments, service groups, industries, and even office locations, none of us heard anything that applied directly to us and our current needs.

No reason to continue watching

By the time they started to address the real reasons for their presentation, most of us had started to mentally wander. Worse yet, the CPA kept turning his back on us to read from the projected slides, while the attorney kept interrupting the CPA to interject "important" points.

Unfortunately, the words on the screen were in a tiny and illegible typeface. Instead of bullet points and single concepts, the presentation was made up of dense paragraphs. Frustrated, quite a few of the audience members began thumbing through the printed handouts, hoping to discover something on point and relevant to what was being said.

Obligatory "runaway train scene" but no hero in sight

 As this conductor-less freight train continued to barrel straight towards oblivion, two professionals seemed oblivious to the disconnect between themselves and the audience. Instead, they made small talk, cracked a few insider jokes, and whirred on, very impressed with themselves. As my mind wandered, I started to think that this could be a script for a B movie, or even for a painful reality television show. Yet, none of it was funny.

Since the two pros had apparently wanted to make sure that they made *every single one* of their points, their presentation ran way over, and very little time was left for questions and answers.

As they wrapped up with closing remarks, and their marketing person began packing away her computer and the remaining plastic imprinted pens that no one had taken, the most senior member of the perspective client's team leaned over to me and said, "Well that was some soliloquy. But I just don't see how it fixes our problems."

Act Two

Several hours later, we reconvened to hear a presentation from another group of professionals. They arrived early, so by the time we walked into the conference room, everything was ready. First of all, this CPA and attorney team had also brought several key players from their respective firms. Before the presentation started, they had walked around and informally introduced everybody to everybody. Interestingly enough, they also seemed to know one or two interesting personal facts about each of us in the room. For instance, one of their senior managers who would be playing a big role in any future work was introduced to one of the perspective client's senior people as a fellow cyclist.

I cannot begin to describe the excitement in these guys' eyes as they got lost in their own world, chatting animatedly about bicycles. This scenario repeated itself several times around the room, as people were connected not just by work, role, and title, but also by areas of *personal* interest.

The energy and excitement in the room was quite high – all this before anything "really" started. When the time arrived for the presentation to begin, people took their seats eager to see what lay ahead. As official introductions began, the screen was covered with vivid images and handfuls of easy to read bullet points. The qualifications of the presenting firms and professionals were covered in terms of how they would likely be an advantage to "us," the perspective client. In fact, the subtle undertone of the entire presentation was, "How *who we are* and *what we do* can help solve *your* problems."

The focus groups worked

It became apparent that long before today's meeting, this team had spoken to the perspective client's senior leadership and had identified a core group of issues to address in their presentation.

Virtual unknowns blow the roof off with fresh, compelling performances

The lead presenters, also a CPA and an attorney, walked us through their slides, rarely turning their backs on us. They didn't trip all over each other, nor did they interrupt each other. While they did not seem scripted, they certainly seemed smooth.

Having their handful of support team members briefly present sections specific to their respective areas of expertise added an additional dimension that the first presenters had lacked. Instead of seeing someone's name and area of expertise flash on the screen, the actual person physically stood up and spoke to us for a few minutes about what they do and how it could benefit us.

Connecting with the audience

Another obvious difference in the presentations was that this second one also used quite a few *very specific* and very appropriate case studies and real life examples. This made it much easier for us, their audience, to understand the value that they would bring to the table. And it also subtly showed us some of the other things that they could potentially do for us if they were hired.

For example, as one of the senior managers described how she and her team conducted on-site audits, she casually added that her firm also provided forensic services that could be of great help in certain situations. Not only had we not known this, we now started thinking of other situations where this expertise could be applied.

Unexpected malfunction almost unnoticed

Halfway through this second presentation, some sort of technological glitch in the boardroom caused the screen to go black. Instead of panicking, the second team continued on, and within moments all of us in the audience quickly forgot about the screen. Their narration of their stories and examples were so on target and so compelling, and they were so diligent in *connecting the dots for us and making sure we would see the value that they brought to us,* that we started to understand exactly how they would solve our problems.

The IT guys fixed the screen glitch just in time for the wrap-up. With plenty of time left for a robust question and answer period, the only real question left was *how can we move forward?*

As the presentation team concluded, they mentioned that our leave-behinds had just been emailed to each of us. As the room began to empty, the interaction and networking continued.

Independent filmmakers triumph over the major studio

At the end of the day, it was strikingly clear that even though the second team of presenters had not been the front-runners, nor did they have the high profile reputations of the first team, they were far better prepared and seemed far more committed to helping us. In fact, not only had they *given* that appearance of commitment, but they *demonstrated* it throughout their presentation.

And *that* was the linchpin. *Demonstration.*

From our perspective, we had expected none of this. Frankly, that morning, we were ready to hire the first crew. Big names, fame, reputation, and all that jazz.

Yet there was something so incredibly compelling about that second presentation that we were drawn in. Once we had been shown the tremendous value that they offered, and realized how much prep work they had done to understand us, we were completely sold. In the timeframe of about an hour, the second set of presenters had dominated over a "sure thing."

The nuts and bolts that make it all work

Now that the stage has been set, let's spend the rest of our time together exploring techniques, tricks, and secrets that will allow you to gain an advantage over the unprepared.

Join along as you learn to add more planning and thought to your approach. See how methods used to take movies and shows and make them blockbusters can also be used by you to make your presentations memorable as well. Then, reap the rewards as you craft your messaging for maximum impact.

You'll also discover tactics that can propel you past those lackluster "sure-thing" firms that are taking presentation-time for granted.

In the end, you will see presentations for what they really are – opportunities to connect and build the trust necessary to close the deal, while being professional and memorable.

The difference between a movie star and a movie actor is this - a movie star will say, "How can I change the script to suit me?" and a movie actor will say. "How can I change me to suit the script?"

Michael Caine

The script – your presentation

Will your presentation be a report? A computerized slide show? A video? Or how about a mixture? Whatever you decide on, be guided by what you feel will work best with your client. Make some calls to determine what the prospect has responded well to in the past. Find out what has worked and what hasn't. And find out why. Also keep in mind that you need to temper your enthusiasm with what you can actually *pull off* based on your available resources and time frame. It is far more important to get to the meeting with a presentation that is 85% there, than to be unable to deliver a coherent presentation since you are over extended trying to create materials you are inept at developing.

A game-changer

Successful pros will often stack the odds for success based on the script. They don't guess at what a prospect wants to see in the presentation. Instead, they find out. They call the prospect before the meeting and ask them *what those attending the meeting* would prefer to see and learn about.

Often, this can be a *game-changing* tactic.

If you can get good detailed answers, you can then tailor your approach to make sure to cover their key points. Maybe they want to know if partners sign up clients and then are rarely heard from again. Maybe they are sensitive to previous overbilling fiascos and need to understand how your firm handles bills. Maybe they need reassurances that you value deadlines as much as they do. In any case, when you address their key concerns as part of your presentation, you are light-years ahead of competitors who are walking in with generic scripts.

Rewrites aren't just common, they are expected

Scripts are often rewritten many times. Then directors will sometimes reinvent scenes "on the fly." Actors will often suggest new dialogue or add other relevant content. What looked good on paper might not translate well, so tweaks are made.

Take the same ownership over your presentation and be fearless about making adjustments that will make the whole effort so much better. Just because something is in writing doesn't mean it's written in stone. Yes, it takes effort. But it could very well spell the difference between a success story and a flop.

Along the same lines *fear not the edit*. If key parts of your presentation *don't sell you to the client* or *don't contain a benefit*—cut cut cut. The worst thing is for the audience to sit immersed in an ocean of "so what?" thoughts as you drone on.

Think "short" and get to the point faster

Use only as much dialogue as necessary to make your points. Make sure your script follows a logical formula. You're telling a story, after all. Make your transitions from scene to scene smooth and easy to follow.

If you are using slides, each slide should *set up* the next, just like each scene should set up the next scene. Set up your action scenes carefully, but don't overdo it. Give your audience places to rest and absorb what they have just heard.

With pictures and graphic elements, only use what supports your words and story. Carefully prune out any distracting visual elements.

Connect the dots and leave nothing to chance. It may help you to read your script out loud to see how it flows. As you are writing your script you should be defining who will play what parts and write to their particular strengths.

Universal is better

For the more tech-savvy amongst you, keep in mind that tying your work to a specific technology limits its effectiveness. Also, software and operating system versions can add a host of challenges. Since your actual presentation may end up being shared on a Mac®, a PC, an android, an iPhone®, a tablet, or anything in between, it is important to make sure that the basic *elements* of your presentation work well on any delivery platform. Better to be more universal than exclusionary. You never want to hear, "I couldn't open it on my PC…"

How to handle loads of data.

So your "director" is married to presenting a ton of data. And no amount of negotiation has been able to dissuade anyone.

First, try to provide that data in leave-behinds, as bound reports, as electronic files on flash drives sporting your logo, or via email. To project spreadsheets on a screen is lunacy. If certain key metrics are the real focus, then a slide that highlights that number and uses the rest of the chart as a backdrop works well.

Consider using large visual graphs with key numbers that are bold and highlighted. Use callouts of key numbers to draw attention. Zoom in to relevant sections. Bullet point the key facts.

Whatever you end up doing, tell your story simply and clearly. It will be far better than projecting tables of endless numbers in microscopic font sizes.

One of the bar associations, at which I taught Continuing Legal Education (CLE) classes, had "presentation slide" rules that went something like this:

- use easy-to-read fonts only
- use bulleted lists instead of paragraphs wherever possible
- no more than 3 points per slide
- type face 32 pts. or larger
- no unnecessary slides
- put the "details" in the handouts

I would add:

- make only one main point per slide
- use only a few action words for each bullet
- avoid swirling text, sliding headlines, and anything else that detracts from your message or theme
- make sure your special effects work flawlessly and are worth the effort

Great advice that should be common sense by now, but isn't.

So now that you have begun to develop your script, let's think about the specific actors you'll want to use – your cast.

The biggest mistake in student films is that they are usually cast so badly, with friends and people the directors know.

Brian De Palma

Casting - picking the team

Brian DePalma's observation is spot-on. Just because "they" are your family and friends, that doesn't mean you immediately stick them in your "movie." Nepotism or favoritism rarely serves you well.

The morning of the presentation is not the time to dole out roles. Research your topic, your prospect, and your approach to make sure you pick your team wisely. If you are solo, the team task is a bit easier (hopefully, you'll choose to take yourself at a minimum).

But who else needs to go? And why? Unless a team member adds value to the effort, why should he go?

Whoever you choose to populate your team, they all need a defined role. Sometimes, a team needs an elder statesman, a subject matter expert, or a simplifier who can explain the concepts in practical terms.

It could be very useful to physically have those people playing key *support roles* at the presentation. It may also be effective to introduce them via short videos that almost feel live. (When you are looking to put your best foot forward, until technology catches up, I still recommend against *going live* over the internet with team intros during *initial* presentations.... it's too risky in terms of service and technology failures, and other glitches like flickering screens, pixilation, and audio delays.)

Video vs. static visuals

Using professionally edited video to paint pictures, introduce team members, and highlight strengths and benefits will propel you past competitors who may be showing only awkward staged executive headshots.

Presentation team vs. Service team

While you choose the service team based on what works best to *service* the client, choose the actual presentation team with the same amount of care – except choose those people that you feel will "click" well with your audience.

Don't make the mistake of feeling that you must include everyone on your service team on your presentation team too.

For your presentation, you are looking to cast only the people that will *resonate best* with your audience – your prospective client. If that includes service team members, great. If not, great.

What next?

So, you've put together a presentation that you feel is your best shot at wooing the prospect. It is professional, neat, error-free, and reflects well on you and your firm. You have also chosen a top-notch presentation team.

Now it is time to choose who will present what parts of the presentation. To be successful, you must consider:

- Who will act as lead team member (emcee)?
- Who will go over the firm history, resources, and stats?
- Who will introduce the team members?

- Who has credibility with the prospect, if anyone?
- Who will do the proposed solution part?
- Who will field fee and pricing questions?
- What about the wrap-up? Who will end?
- Who will set expectations and outline the next steps?
- Who will go for a soft close, if any?

Once people are assigned responsibility for the above roles and actions, it's time to move on to the read-through.

Every time I get a script it's a matter of trying to know what I could do with it. I see colors, imagery. It has to have a smell. It's like falling in love. You can't give a reason why.

Paul Newman

The read-through

One direction

With responsibility assigned to various presentation team members for various parts and tasks, now is the time to get all the team members on the "same page" by doing a thorough read-through of the presentation.

A read-through yields many benefits including the ability to test-drive sound and meaning, actors, voices, pronunciations, the completeness of the script, and more. Further, when used to its full potential, a read-through can become a brain storming session on steroids. The *key* is for the director to maintain an open mind and be willing to craft and recraft what truly is, at this point, a work in progress.

How it *really* sounds...

It is absolutely amazing how different words can "sound" when they are spoken, not silently read. What you thought was prose worthy of Shakespeare while in print suddenly sounds like complete dry dribble during your read-through.

Speaking the presentation affords you the luxury of true emphasis, innuendo, and loads of passion with which written word just can't compete. A read-through will allow you to gage if what you thought you were conveying in writing is *actually being conveyed* when spoken.

Let's not forget the entertainment aspect of any presentation.

Since many of us professionals learned to write in a very dry and factual style, a read-through will serve to identify those areas that may need an injection of life. Yes, yes, I agree that you need to maintain professionalism… but you don't have to be boring!

Location really doesn't matter

Where you do your read-through is far less important than how you do it. I've directed effective read-throughs in a wide variety of locales including hotel rooms, boardrooms, living rooms, airplanes, via video conferencing, and outdoors on picnic tables.

The key is to go through the presentation, from start to finish, with everyone presenting their respective parts as they come up.

It is vital to assign a team member to take notes so that any changes, refinements, or other brilliant ideas that emerge from the session are not lost.

Setting the stage for a read-through

Great Hollywood directors have been known to begin read-throughs by painting a picture of the story, reminding the actors of the context of the tale, the historical setting, what has happened to other characters just prior to the opening scene, and asking for the emotions that they expect.

Similarly, you should always open with an overview. Paint the big picture for your team. Then make it clear what their *individual* roles will mean to the effort. Be sure to cover the following:

- What will the presentation cover?
- What form will it take (audiovisual, collateral)?
- How much time has been allocated?
- Where will it be held?
- Who will the audience likely be?
- What concerns might the perspective client have?
- What questions are they inclined to ask?
- What's the goal of the presentation?
- What do you want to walk away with?

Add anything else that will better prepare those who are rehearsing to shine and excel.

Transitions

Before you read through, decide if team members will hand off sections *formally* – "That is the end of my section. May I introduce my associate Jane Doe who will take us through the next section." – or *informally* – by simply sitting down while the next presenter starts. Or, maybe you'll choose my favorite technique which centers around the team leader serving as the "emcee" for the entire meeting, handling all introductions and transitions, and connecting all the dots. This "storyteller" style can be the most powerful way to present when done right.

Are cast members living up to their roles?

As you proceed with the read-through, critique the performance (or lack thereof) of your prospective presenters. Now is the time to encourage, coach, or replace presenters. If during the read-through a critical team member turns out to be a terrible presenter but needs to be at the presentation "no matter what," then at least you know what you are up against *now* and can whittle down their "on-screen" time as much as possible.

How much should be memorized?

Memorizing exact paragraphs is not recommended. Then again, ad-libbing can be as good as it can be bad. Without a teleprompter, even the president of the United States can be at a loss for words. Make sure everyone is clear on their main points. Rather than rote memorization, it is often good to memorize only key concepts and then "work around them" with your own words.

Make sure that each presenter understands his or her individual role as well as how they fit into the whole presentation. This is especially important in case someone forgets a key point. When everybody understands the main goal, any of the presenters can add in a forgotten point or even pick up on it later so that it is not lost.

We're all set now, right?

Well, you *are* closer.

Remember the two pros from the introduction that blew their big opportunity? There is a lot more to presenting than showing up.

Now it is time to rehearse, rehearse, and rehearse.

Rehearsals

At least one, if not several full-length rehearsals should be done to iron out all the glitches, transitions, and general flow.

During your rehearsal, keep an eye on delivering a complete story. Since the presentation should tell a tale from beginning to end and come to a logical and satisfying conclusion, it is important not to have cliffhangers – no *first part* of a trilogy. Instead of ending on a confusing or murky note that lends itself to misinterpretation, you want to wrap up with all the good guys triumphing over the bad guys.

Follow Hollywood's lead and have your hero's brilliance and aptitude save your client's day!

Inject energy in appropriate levels

If you're not passionate about your message, why expect your audience to be interested?

As Hollywood icon Robert Redford once said, "… get emotionally connected to your story so you can deliver it, you know, if you can't deliver the emotions to your script there's no point to your story."

Inject energy. Inject passion. Let your audience *feel* your commitment and expertise. Just don't overdo it. Pace yourself. You aren't looking for maximum volume throughout the entire presentation. Choose your points of emphasis, as well as your crescendos, carefully. You need peaks and valleys to make your story engaging and *memorable.*

Respect everyone's time and stick to schedules

At many firms, billable time "rules." Thus, getting people together to rehearse several times, *let alone once,* can be challenging. Therefore, it is vital that everyone understands the importance of rehearsing together and that they make that commitment.

An unstructured attitude towards rehearsals is a sure way to alienate the true professionals among your team. Those top performers will be the first to acknowledge the importance for rehearsing. But waste their time, and they'll be the first to bail out or avoid doing it next time.

For time to be well spent, be sure that *rehearsal time* is tightly controlled – start on time, end promptly, agree on next steps, and move on.

Once you think that your presentation is smooth and pretty close to a "final cut," it's time for a *private screening.*

Do this next part right and you will be able to stack the odds for your success by gauging audience reaction and comprehension way in advance of the actual presentation date.

No one leaves the edit room thinking, 'Yeah, I nailed that one!' Everyone I know goes into their first premiere or their first screening thinking, 'I screwed up so bad. I'm sorry, I messed up.' It's just a real common feeling.

Mike Mills

Private screenings – getting feedback

Forget about eyeball movement monitors, EKGs, and a host of other scientific gadgets used by high-tech audience research laboratories. Realistically, you should plan to do your proposed presentation *at least once* for an audience that will provide smart feedback.

Doing a practice presentations in front of a few trusted advisors, your screening audience, can yield insights that will help you to fine-tune all aspects of your "show." From identifying timing issues to clarifying content to suggestions for a stronger close, your audience can provide some worthwhile suggestions that people much more involved in the project may no longer be able to see.

The makeup of the screening audience is key. Ideally, you want a mix of professionals who

A) understand presentation dynamics,
B) are familiar with industry or industries involved,
C) aren't envious of *or antagonistic towards* the presenters
D) approximate the demographics of the perspective client's audience, and
E) will tell you what they *really* think.

33

For instance, if you were preparing a presentation for professional services aimed at a relatively young startup of mostly 20- and 30-something year old entrepreneurs, then you'd want your screening audience to include a few people that match that demographic. Generational insight and perspective can make for some truly interesting comments.

Missing the forest for the trees

Sometimes, professionals are so invested in their presentation that it can be difficult to see the obvious. Other times, professionals are so bent on making certain points that they fail to address the "elephant in the client's room"? A certain amount of groupthink (where members of a group blindly support their group without any critique) may creep in as well.

Your screening audience can serve as your safety net.

Before you begin the presentation

Prior to launching into the presentation, take a few minutes to make everyone attending the "screening" aware of *your* goals as well as the *perspective client's* needs and wants. Ask audience members to make notes on anything that creates "a disconnect" for them as they view your presentation.

It works best if you perform your presentation as if it were the *real thing*, from start to finish. Don't stop and chat with the screening audience and then pick up again only to make comments to others in the room and then engage in unrelated sidebars, et cetera…

Probe to get to the core

Once the presentation is completed, a thoughtful discussion with your screening audience will help you determine areas to improve. The question, "So what did you think?" rarely gets at the heart of the matter without significant probing. Ask specific questions, and then follow-up with questions to uncover any areas that need to be addressed. Just like with the calculated cross-examinations of witnesses, remember to ask for specifics.

Examples of questions you might ask your screening audience include:

- Based on our presentation, what do you think was our most important point that we were trying to make?
- What would you guess is the client's main concern based on what we emphasized in our presentation?
- Did we convey our ability to help the client?
- What specifically did you think got that point across?
- Did the audio visuals support or detract?
- What was missing?
- Were you able to follow along?
- Did anything confuse you?
- How were the transitions?
- What seemed like fluff or filler?
- Was anything not credible?

Of course, you need to take any and all comments and feedback with that famous "grain of salt." You can't, and shouldn't, have to try to please everyone.

Yet often you may find that even one or two observations that reveal hidden or missed opportunities could easily be incorporated into the final presentation and could be the difference between succeeding or not.

Cinema is a matter of what's in the frame
and what's out.

Martin Scorsese

The cutting room floor

Professionals have a tendency to throw absolutely everything they can into their presentations. Many become an endless string of "and we can…", "and we also…", "and we are…"

After your private screening, it will be a wonderful time to shed the fat. Cut out the fluff. Eliminate anything that distracts and dismays, while bolstering up those qualifications and points that directly speak to the prospective client's needs and concerns.

On the subject of the "screening feedback," this is *not* an exact science. Don't feel compelled to make every suggested change! You want to improve *your* presentation – not end up with *their* presentation. Work to retain *your* unique style and flair while considering *their* best critiques.

Further, look at how practical it will be to implement a suggestion. Sometimes it isn't worth reprinting or redesigning volumes of material for a minor item. Other times, it makes all the difference in the world – such as in the case of a firm that spent thousands of dollars reprinting materials at the last minute when they realized that they had missed a typo that identified their team of professionals as *certified **pubic** accountants.*

Now let's learn some ways to create winning environments that help sell *you*.

I'm the kind of person who likes to create the environment and mindset - not because I do it deliberately, but because that's how I like to live - where, from catering to makeup to hair to wardrobe, electricians, camera department lighting, sound, you know, it's our movie; we're together, and we have that camaraderie and that closeness.

Steve McQueen

Creating the environment

One of my signatures is to create memorable environments. From stadiums to mansions to offices to boardrooms, I've produced a multitude of settings aimed at evoking specific feelings and emotions with one goal in mind: to connect with my audience in a memorable way.

If your meeting space is your canvas, how will you personalize it and make it not only memorable, but also your own?

Some of my favorite ways to make my mark include:

- using branded candy for the meeting table
- having branded note pads and imprinted pens waiting at each audience member's seat
- setting up bold branded pop-up signage that features key strategic messaging that subliminally "stares" at the audience throughout the presentation
- projecting a high-tech video loop with a strategic message prior to the presentation

- playing specially selected background music for certain meetings prior to and after the actual presentation
- syncing real-time photography that melds the audience right into our onscreen presentation
- projecting our logo with the audience's logo intertwined in a deliberate way on specific items that imply that the "marriage" is not only the right decision, but that it is the best decision as well
- creating and walking clients through mock-ups of typical work products that they can expect from us, that are dually branded, with subliminal triggers and content

The meeting environment can be further hedged by asking for and creating a warm and cordial networking segment for about 10 minutes prior to launching into your presentation. Always call ahead and clear this activity as many prospective clients are used to simply showing up at exactly the appointed time (or even a few minutes late) and sitting down.

If challenged as to why you want to do this networking session, simply answer with some version of

> "in the age of over-electrified communications, my firm still values the human end of things… since a good working relationship based on mutual respect and trust is one of the keys to our success, we like to start by briefly connecting on a human level, before jumping into the data… we appreciate meeting the people behind the bios…"

While you can't always control or influence your presentation environment as much as you would like, your wardrobe is 110% all yours. Read on.

Wardrobe – the look that helps sell your story

Imagine you're watching a movie about General Patton and the actor performing the part is in Bermuda shorts and a t-shirt. Would you be buying his performance, no matter how impressive?

Along these lines, are you dressing *your* part? Are you conveying a sense of professionalism that inspires trust and believability?

Anticipation and perception

Put yourself in the prospect's shoes.

As a prospective client who is considering spending hundreds of dollars or more per hour for your expertise, I really need to see you reflect what I am investing in.

Accordingly, my *anticipation* is that you will *look* like the successful professional I want to hire to represent me. Once I meet you, I will (knowingly or unknowingly) form a *perception* of who you are based on your wardrobe.

Buttoned-up *trumps* frumpy, every time

While some may think that they should dress exactly like their audience, and some consultants have endless opinions on this

39

matter, I *strongly* suggest that you dress the part that you are auditioning for – the trusted advisor to the prospect.

Taking into account any regional idiosyncrasies, dress at the level that what would be considered *formal business attire* in your area.

But they told us it was casual Friday

What if they perspective client calls to tell you that they are dressing in *business casual* on the day of your presentation?

So what?

If you are portraying a successful attorney, then you should *look* like a successful attorney. If they are expecting to meet with highly regarded accountants, then that is what you should deliver.

Once you win the account and have proven yourself, then it may be time to revisit your dress code when visiting or meeting with the client. Even so, many top professionals I work with rarely dress down.

The nightclub look

I hope I don't have to explain this, but huge rings, fat wrist chains of gold, silk suits, and designer ties may scream "overpriced egoist" louder than "successful professional."

Again, for most situations, somewhat more conservative and professional attire, *not gaudy attire*, will serve you well.

Spinning your wheels

As far as your "ride" is concerned, I've heard arguments on both sides of the fence. Some prospective clients expect a successful professional to be driving an expensive car. Others may feel it shows extravagant taste or, worse yet, a propensity to over-charge.

If you are unsure, go for something in the middle when visiting clients and keep the monster sports car for private time. The last thing you want is for the prospect, or *client* for that matter, to look at her staff and say, "I don't intend to help pay for his Porsche!" (True story.) And once the prospective client starts to fixate on fees *and not results*, your road is all downhill. Proceed at your own risk.

Next, in true Hollywood fashion, we will explore props, leave-behinds, and even special effects.

The three basic types of properties are stage props, such as furniture, news desks, and lecterns; set dressings, such as pictures, draperies, and lamps, and hand props, which are items such as dishes, telephones, and typewriters actually handled by the talent.

Television Production Handbook, 5th edition
by Herbert Zettl,

Props and equipment – the tools of the trade

When used effectively, props almost disappear into the background. They help the story along, build credibility, and *never* detract from your message.

My advice on props and equipment is to be as self-sufficient as possible. How many times have meetings been delayed since someone didn't know that a projector, or screen, or certain type of computer was needed? Assume nothing and bring your entire production on the road with you – electronics, speakers, extension cables, and all.

And have a Plan B. *Plenty of Plan Bs.* No wall space to project the images? No problem, let's watch it on our over-sized screen laptop. Internet connection out today? No worries, we have mobile Wi-Fi. Glitch with the network cable? No sweat, let's review the screen shots we prepared. Copier not available? No issues since we have extra handouts.

What props or equipment do you need, if any, to make your production the best it can be?

You don't need a big close, as many sales reps believe. You risk losing your customer when you save all the good stuff for the end. Keep the customer actively involved throughout your presentation, and watch your results improve.

Harvey Mackay

The leave-behind

You have worked hard to make sure that your presentation is a strong driver of your message, a flattering representation of who you are, and a blueprint for what you are looking to accomplish. This leads to the question of leave-behinds...

The tradition of providing a leave-behind *is a given.*

The format used for that leave-behind *is not.*

The choice used to revolve around a stack of photocopied paper, with binding being the big differentiator – stapled, bound, clipped, in a folder, heat-sealed, et cetera.

Now, the decisions are far more involved...

- do you leave a bound report?
- how about using files on flash drives?
- maybe as an attachment to a follow-up email?
- could you host it as a YouTube® video?
- or, create a place on your website for download?

Whatever you choose to do, in whatever combination of options, keep in mind that everything seems to be passed around, *or forwarded*, endlessly. Unfortunately, people don't usually include any explanation beyond, "Here's the presentation." In anticipation of a similarly lackluster handoff, including some sort of "executive summary" or preamble to any version of your presentation is strongly encouraged.

If you don't "set the tone," someone else will...

In an attempt to better control messaging when they provide copies of their presentations, I advise clients to *always* add a "description" that subtly influences the receiver.

For instance, "The attached is a presentation Able Baker Charley LLP prepared for XYZ Corp. to address their need for a better and more effective way to accomplish year-end tax planning and details the specific advantages that AbleBakerCharley brings to the table, including successful case studies."

Depending on the delivery method, this "description" can take many forms including: email text, cover sheet, text over video, voice-over, file attachment, pdf, et cetera.

Other leave-behind sections that are often overlooked

Apart from the typical information that you will need to include in your leave-behind, here are some *specific thoughts* on sections often not given a *second thought*.

Team bios

Bios for top team members should be balanced and equally robust. If yours is a true team effort, no one member should be made to stand out much more than any other based on physical bio length (number of words), unless you need to make them more prominent as in the case of a true subject matter expert. For less experienced team, members, a smaller amount of bio detail is expected.

Dump the encyclopedia

If you have been filling your presentations with bios that look more like bland encyclopedia entries, it's not your fault. You were probably taught to do that somewhere along the way. But, it is not helping your cause one bit.

Strive to cut the flowery adjectives and concentrate on value. Think in terms of the prospect's point of view. Why would they want... *no*... why would they *insist* on hiring this person after reading his or her bio?

As I explain in my book *Networking Success* (in the Elevator Speech chapter), your goal is to explain succinctly, *in a memorable way,* what value you and your business or service bring to the table.

Here is additional relevant guidance directly from that book:

> Frame your introduction in terms of benefits. Express yourself in plain terms and try to zero in on the kind of clients you want. Don't make your audience work hard to decipher what you bring to the table. Don't make your listeners guess whom they might be able to recommend. This is not the time to throw around vague and broad statements. Better to get a smaller number of targeted referrals rather than lots of off-the-mark time wasters (or no referrals at all).

> Remember a while back we spoke about the power of "third party endorsements"? And you may have

wondered how this would work for an "elevator speech" since *you* are introducing yourself –and you won't have the benefit of a *third* party endorsement? I have found that one of the best ways to give yourself a legitimate "third party endorsement" is to relate what others have said about you in a non-obnoxious way.

For instance, I have heard super networkers give themselves that "outside endorsement" by saying something along the lines of

> "My clients tell me that what they value most about what I bring to the table is …"

Or some version of

> "My client appreciated the results I was able to get for her so much that she immediately referred me to three of her associates…"

Be crisp and professional. Be well versed. You are speaking about what you do. Don't sound tentative or unsure. Don't umm and aww. Be convincing, positive, and confident. And finally, be memorable.

[end of excerpt]

So the take-away here is to rewrite your bios in terms of *why* you and your team members would be valuable to the prospective client. Sure, list the schools, degrees, and titles; add the relevant articles and speeches; and include a few interests or hobbies that you think might resonate with the crowd – just don't forget to think in terms of *your client's* needs and expectations.

Recently, a client of mine really took this concept to heart. She rewrote every one of her presentation bios, and saw immediate positive feedback from prospects. She made herself and her partners more approachable by adding some interesting hobbies and philanthropic pursuits to each bio. Then she also included a few sentences to each person's list of accomplishments aimed at how they had helped a client: "Jane is adept at assisting clients with potential out-of-state residency issues steer clear of trouble, and has helped hundreds successfully challenge ..."

To her surprise, it was actually the bio sections that highlighted "unexpected hobbies" and those that demonstrated "results on behalf of other clients" that prompted the most prospective client interest and discussion.

Headshots need to be *recent*.

I have seen way too many presentations with headshots that were absurdly outdated – you've seen them too – where the pictures no longer look like the people standing in front of you.

Hey, I worked on Madison Avenue. I get it. You want to look your best. But I am not harping on some photo touch up. What makes people nervous is the photo of a bushy haired younger fellow who is standing in right in front of them quite bald. Or, a photo that is at least decade old and some 30 pounds lighter...

Contact information

My final suggestion in this section is to make it *easy* for prospects to contact you. No one should have to hunt for your email, phone number, or web page on your leave-behind. Make that info prominent and *easy* to find.

The technology available for filmmaking now is incredible, but I am a big believer that it's all in the story.

Robert Redford

Special effects – making sure your presentation is memorable

While using too many effects can distract the audience and even end up detracting from your message, some well-executed effects can serve to further your cause and leave a top-notch impression. Especially when you are competing against some equally matched opponents, any little differentiators can help sway the odds in your favor.

Special effects don't have to be epic

Something as simple as easy-to-read financial projections or clear summaries of main points can set you apart from competitors that rely on impossible-to-read slides in ridiculously tiny typeface.

Several well-placed video testimonials or case studies within the presentation have the potential to tip the scales, especially if they are tailored to the specific prospect.

Other "special effects" such as having a video of a partner speaking and walking across a presentation screen or a hand filling in information on a virtual whiteboard certainly can make your presentation memorable. But balance is key.

48

Less can be more

Remember when all PowerPoint® presentations suddenly included:

- that blue background screen?
- swirling or moving text?
- sound effects, like typewriters and applause?
- animated logos that twirled around?

The choices today are truly limitless so while it pays to spice up your presentation, be careful not to overdo it.

Hollywood movies follow that formula perfectly. The audience is always given some time to settle down after an intense scene. There is a carefully orchestrated pattern of peaks and valleys.

So, while special effects have the real opportunity to seal the deal – and to make you memorable – they also can overwhelm the audience, or even desensitize them. Overdoing special effects can make your big scenes seem lackluster and bland.

My rule is to use special effects only when they help to tell your story and solidify your position.

Well, that's pretty much it in a nutshell. See you at opening night!

Opening night – your one and only shot to get rave reviews

Let's switch gears to Broadway for a moment – it is a rare Broadway production that makes it past a poor showing on its opening night.

Poor first impressions are awfully hard to overcome, especially with all the professional services choices that exist. You must strive for a record-breaking first showing. It will likely be your only shot.

So it's time for your premiere. Your team is well rehearsed. You have all your timing down. No one has called in sick, yet.

Here are some ideas to stack the odds for success:

- find out about your presentation room ahead of time
- arrive ½ hour early to set up
- clear your early arrival ahead of time so that there are no surprises (you may not be able to actually get into the presentation room earlier than called for)
- be prepared with contingency plans and backup equipment

- check that you have your presentation on all your electronic devises, and that it opens and works
- my favorite "emergency" supplies include a very long extension cord, an equally long network cable, a roll of duct tape, and a large black marker – as weird as it sounds, these few items have saved the day many *many* times
- while most presentations are now computerized, or Bluetooth® driven, if you will be using a projector of any kind, a spare light bulb is worth its weight in gold
- a set of various charging cables never hurts

Pre-presentation networking

Don't forget that informal pre-presentation networking session. If you can squeeze it in, it's golden. As we saw in the example at the very start of the book, learning about your audience and then speaking with them specifically about those points of connection, such as hobbies, interests, schools attended, can really create the backdrop for a memorable presentation. Here's where it really pays to know your audience and know it well. A little bit of internet research may uncover quite a lot about them.

Lighting

During the actual presentation, make sure that the lighting in the room is not too dim. You don't want to risk people drifting off.

Volume

Pay attention to "volume." And not just the volume of the voices of those presenting. Make sure that any audio that is part of your presentation is clearly heard from any position throughout the room. A great message or point that is not heard is useless.

Alternatively, don't crank the volume too high and distort your message. Be alert.

Movement

Hopefully, you've already realized you shouldn't be fidgeting, jiggling coins in your pockets, playing with any jewelry, clicking pens, chewing gum, snapping fingers, swaying, bouncing your leg or legs up and down, smacking lips, dribbling or slurping drinks, scratching, or nervously tapping on anything.

Any of this unnecessary motion can easily distract your audience. It may even make some people feel anxious or nervous. Guard against anything that lessens focus.

Hand motions can, and should, be used to underscore points you're making. But don't flap unnecessarily.

Facial expressions

During the presentation, don't forget to smile – as appropriate. However, if you're delivering particularly bad or sad news, this is not the time to laugh or smirk. Whatever the circumstances, pay particular attention to exude an aura of confidence and professionalism.

This goes for your entire team as well. As one member is presenting, the rest of the team should be focused on the presentation and supporting it with positive body language, good posture, and attentive gaze.

Unforgivable offenses

Under no circumstance should *any* of your team members be texting, emailing, or otherwise using an electronic or other device not related to the presentation. Period.

Audience feedback

All team members should be monitoring the audience for agreement or confusion, attention or boredom. On-the-fly adjustments should be made accordingly. If a particularly tedious part of the presentation is just not working, you may make an executive decision to summarize it and move past it.

If you sense some serious disinterest, it also doesn't hurt to ask the perspective client if he or she would like you to continue expanding upon certain sections of your presentation or if they are more interested in other sections that you could substitute or move towards immediately.

Customizing your presentation on the fly, as you are presenting, is not the easiest thing to do, but sometimes it just makes sense.

The question of questions

Have you ever been at a presentation and a point is made that gets your mind wandering? Or worse yet, did something strike you as so odd, or so out of the ordinary, that you literally couldn't refocus? How did that work out for you?

Interrupting the presentation for questions is not a great idea. It's often advantageous to have all questions held to the end.

But sometimes audience members may be so caught up on some part of your presentation that they either didn't understand, didn't agree with, or simply flat out misinterpreted that they have actually disconnected. They start to fidget or stare or seem bothered. Addressing them, especially if they are a key decision maker, is essential. Better to stop the presentation, answer their concerns, and move on, than to let something fester and ruin their ability to follow along.

How do you handle forgotten lines or missed cues?

Since you are in front of a "live studio audience," anything can happen. Whenever Jackie Gleason forgot a line during the recording of his *Honeymooners* live television show many years ago, he would rub his stomach or put his finger into his front jacket pocket. Alert cast members would jump in and ad-lib until Jackie was back on track. The audience never realized what was happening, and some of those ad-libs became classic moments.

So, if you realize a team member has "gotten lost" or has forgotten a cue, assist as *imperceptibly* as possible. The idea is for the show to go on without the audience noticing.

While it is critical for the presentation team to stay alert so that they can help out as necessary. However, this is *not* license to interrupt, interject, or to do anything else that will only disrupt the presentation and make people nervous.

If you see that a team member needs help, then help! Just do it suavely…

What if we sense that we are losing the audience?

There are no hard and fast rules

Sometimes, you may feel that for the sake of your presentation you need to clear the air and ask questions right on the spot.

Frame the questions in terms of *trying to better serve them,* rather than making them feel (whether intentionally or not) that you are superior to them.

For instance, try:

- What we were trying to say was_____. Is that how it came across?

as opposed to:

- "You look confused..."
- "Can't you see that..."
- "What part of this don't you understand..."

Avoid these latter approaches that are loaded with negative implications.

The aim of any question you ask, as a presenter, should be to *clarify* and move forward in a *positive* light. Follow this rule and you will come off as concerned that the audience is getting the most value from the presentation, instead of irritated at their inability to grasp your genius...

While you don't want to let confusion fester, remember that you can't allow the presentation to get sidetracked either. It's a tight balance, no matter how much presenting experience you have or don't have.

Sometimes clients will file into a room and sit at attention. Other times, people will randomly flow in and out. I would suggest you do your best to keep on track. If you feel it necessary, you may even ask new arrivals if they want a recap of the presentation up to that point.

What if the top prospect leaves the meeting?

If the person you've identified as the key stakeholder suddenly leaves the room, it is definitely time to do some fancy footwork. If there was some excuse given, then accept it and march forward. If that person left without a word, ask the remaining attendees whether you should continue or wait for that key stakeholder's return. Depending upon the answer you get, figure out your next move, which is almost *always* to stay the course.

I have rarely seen a presentation stop completely because the top person exited. Maybe they've seen enough to be satisfied that you're "it," or "not it." Maybe they got bored. Maybe they are going to let the rest of their group make the decision and simply wanted to get a feel for your team.

Whatever the case, stay calm and present on…

Remember the kid that didn't thank you for coming to their birthday party?

Once questions and answers have been completed and your presentation is finished, remember to verbally thank each attendee for making the time to meet with you. Good manners, a can-do attitude, and a confident handshake will work wonders especially when the competition is tight.

As I say in my chapter on "Signals" in my Networking Success book, "your handshake may be the only physical contact that you have with the other person. Research shows that it definitely creates a specific impression on the other person, whether it is subtle or not. To stack the odds for your success, you want to go for a firm and confident handshake."

How about swag? Promotional stuff?

Beyond the simple "thank you," a Hollywood technique at premieres and similar events is the *swag bag* filled with branded items all linked to the movie or occasion.

While there is certainly no obligation to do anything, I've seen all sorts of items that run the gamut from imprinted high-end pens, doorman umbrellas, and calculators, to flash drives, baseball caps, iPods®, and candy holders – all emblazoned with some combination of logo, web address, and contact info.

Does it have to be a pen?

Not at all!

Resourceful alternatives to the "corporate pen" include presenting the prospects with a custom created "new trends report" for their industry, or an invitation to a seminar on a pertinent topic that they would find valuable – anything specialized that would *extend the conversation* and prolong the initial relationship beyond the presentation.

While these branded items may or may not set you apart, the way you give them to prospective clients certainly will. Putting one gift-wrapped item (wrapped in paper featuring your logo) in front of each attendee's place *prior* to the meeting starting is far better than leaving a heaping loose pile in the middle of the table.

Handing a wrapped item to each attendee as you are leaving and thanking them for their time and attention is better than just leaving a stack of stuff for them to pick through.

Two observations:

  a) People of any age still love to unwrap stuff, and
  b) Classy is classy.

We now move on to a critical piece of the process – follow-up.

Initial follow-up

Even after a terrific opening night, it is essential to follow up with some key maneuvers designed to strengthen your position.

Always contact the prospect after the meeting and thank them for their time and consideration. Reiterate that you are "more convinced than ever" that your firm would be the perfect choice to get the work done. Add a few smart observations that the meeting has allowed you to make. End with a comment about your continued excitement and commitment to their project and an invitation to actively pursue next steps.

Follow up by phone within a short period of time. Don't overwhelm them, but definitely don't grow cold. Ask if there is anything else that you could *do* or *prepare* for them to help in their decision making process.

Open and *clear* communications are key at this stage.

If you sense that they are falling out of love, see what can be done to rekindle the flame. Yet, don't smother or stalk.

Ideas on how to follow-up after you find out you weren't chosen

Sometimes a match seems so right that it is baffling you aren't attached at the hip. But, if your best efforts have yielded nothing, move on – just don't give up. And don't simply fade away. The fact that you had been included on a short list is already good.

After officially *not being picked*, find occasional reasons to reach out. At a minimum, ask for permission to add them to your marketing email list. Regular newsletters, email alerts, and event invitations will keep you on the radar especially since things always change. But, again, don't be a stalker.

Stack the odds for *future* success by leaving things off in a very positive way. Instead of revealing loads of disappointment or lamenting your lost time, encourage revisits by saying something along the lines of:

"Well, it seemed to all of us that we were perfect for each other, but for whatever reason it wasn't meant to be this time around. However, since no one has the monopoly on good ideas, let's stay in touch because you never know when you might want to re-explore your options. I invite you to always feel free to reach out to us."

Hey, you made it to their finals – so staying in touch can reap big rewards, specifically when the other firm fails to live up to expectations or outlives their capabilities.

This is particularly important if you were a "close contender" yet lost on price alone. Here's why. Let's agree you did a fair and accurate job of estimating hours and costs. To come in much lower, a firm in your league may have underestimated the hours or costs, or they may have intentionally underbid in order to "buy" the business.

In either case, as their billings begin to creep (or speed) up, *and they always do,* don't be surprised if you get a second chance at that account *if you have followed my suggestions* and stayed in touch.

The benefit to this approach is that when you get that call to revisit, you are in a far stronger position than before.

Nice…

Bowling scenes tend to pop up in films that fizzle...Therefore it is statistically unwise to include one in your script.

Vinny Bruzzese, Hollywood script consultant, interviewed by Brooks Barnes, New York Times

The Debriefing Meeting

Chosen or rejected, a debriefing meeting is essential!

A debriefing meeting should be held soon after the actual presentation while the details are still fresh. It doesn't have to be a long and drawn out affair. But look carefully at the entire presentation *from the client's perspective*. It is good to have all the team members present. Some of the most valuable comments may very well come from younger or less involved members of the team, since they might be less jaded or drunk with "groupthink."

Make the meeting meaningful

After the team leader opens with a very brief overview of the presentation's goals and the prospective client's perceived and/or stated needs, every member of the team should get the same amount of time to comment and weigh in. Go over each key aspect of the effort, from the planning to the execution.

A small sample of questions I like to ask includes:

- in retrospect, did we really understand the prospective client as well as we thought we did going in?

61

- were we on target with our presentation?
- was it long enough? Too long?
- what was the reaction? Why?
- what did we do to exceed the client's expectations?
- what can we surmise from the Q&A?
- what questions did we not expect?
- how were our transitions?
- did anyone talk too much? Not enough?
- was anyone making strange noises, movements, or causing a distraction?
- how many "umm umm umms" were there?
- did the audiovisual go as planned?
- what felt clumsy? What worked better than expected?
- did the presentation flow well?
- what should we have included that we didn't?
- what was overdone, if anything?
- what did we learn from this as a team? Individually?
- what can we do more of? What can we change?
- what do we need to stop doing?
- how can we apply what we learned to the next presentation?
- et cetera, et cetera…

The team leader *must* be sure to keep particularly vociferous members at bay. No one learns when one or two strong personalities hijack a debriefing meeting. It has to be a team effort.

Protect freedom of speech

People must feel that they will not be stigmatized or slandered later on for their honest opinions. Without this sense of safety to freely express their observations, people will often revert to a much safer "everything was good" mentality and *that* is a complete waste of everyone's time.

There's always one...

Once, part way through what could have been a break-through debriefing meeting, a decrepit, nasty, know-it-all member (who had fallen flat at the presentation being discussed) began taking up all of the time and spotlight to pontificate about nonsense, while he blamed less experienced team members for real and imagined failings. There wasn't an ounce of constructive dialogue.

Within moments, team members were not only demotivated (one subsequently quit to go to another firm, and another moved to a different niche group), but no one in the debriefing meeting grew personally or professionally that day.

Worse yet, the know-it-all began a personal vendetta against several of the members that had mentioned some things he didn't like during the meeting. A wonderful opportunity *to get better* was gone in a puff of chatter.

Find out "what makes your presentations fizzle?"

There are many reasons for not getting picked. Beyond the obvious, sometimes it is just a culmination of many little things that added up to "no." Some explanations are subtle, yet some may even be nefarious.

Among the endless collection of "turn down reasons" are:

- personalities just didn't mesh
- you rubbed someone the wrong way
- you didn't portray a professional enough image
- another presentation seemed more compelling

- the fix was in, and a friend of a friend was already "in"
- your team seemed unprepared
- your audiovisual was dated
- you were just the obligatory "one of three" estimates
- someone didn't answer a basic question smoothly
- a team member copped a better than thou attitude
- the team looked sloppy
- someone displayed a know-it-all complex
- there was too much talking and not enough listening
- someone wore a tie and no socks
- someone wore a strange big hat and no tie

Whatever the case, seek to determine the causes and correct them for the next time. Here is where honesty, *not blame*, will work wonders. Team members must share info and analyze themselves, and each other, honestly in order to learn *and grow* from the experience.

Learn as much as you can and march on

Learn everything you can from each presentation. Weigh the feedback (keeping in mind that not all feedback is relevant), filter out what is useful, discard the garbage, and make the necessary and practical corrections. Then, march on.

No beating yourself, or anyone else, up. No dwelling on what *might* have been.

One of your goals is always to be improving at presenting, and always to be looking for ways to make your presentations better. So learn what you can, make the adjustments, but ultimately, spend your energy on finding the next opportunity and then the next and … march on!

A Few Final Thoughts

Based on many years devoted to training professionals to *up their game* when making presentations, here are some of the additional hints that I would have called "common sense" a while back, but I now highlight:

- DO rehearse to the point that you sound *un*rehearsed. (Read that again.)
- DO go for a natural and conversational delivery
- DO take a public speaking course if you feel you want to be more at ease when presenting
- DO take a moment to explain technical terms and acronyms rather than risk a confused audience
- DO take younger firm members to key presentations occasionally as it really helps them to develop
- DON'T smoke or eat pungent foods such as onion, garlic, scallions, curry, et cetera, prior to presenting
- DON'T forget to listen for what is really concerning your prospective clients

Ultimately, you are the author of your success.

Learning new techniques and being exposed to new tools is great, but actually APPLYING them appropriately and consistently is essential.

So, take the best of the ideas to which you are exposed and pick out *and implement* what works for you.

Start today!

Some additional valuable excerpts especially for professionals to peruse

An excerpt from the book

OFFICIAL BUSINESS DEVELOPMENT SERIES
for Professionals
How to Make Your Firm a Better Place Than You Found It

But I'm too busy to market....

A common feeling that professionals have about "marketing" is that somehow it encroaches on their "serious" time. It is seen as an annoyance, and even a disruption, to getting billable work done.

If you see "marketing" as an unrelated task for which you need to stop your world to plow through… then yes, marketing is all the bad things you've thought it to be. But it is so, because of the way you have decided to approach it, define it, and execute it.

When done right, marketing actually becomes second nature and melds seamlessly into daily activities. It takes almost no extra effort and causes no grand disruptions.

For instance, if you train yourself to spend the first 10 - 15 minutes of every day sending cards or notes or information to the people you met or socialized with the day before, then marketing hasn't been annoying. If you set aside some time at the end of each day to scan publications of interest to your clients for timely info that they would be interested in, then marketing hasn't disrupted anything. It could actually be a welcome break from the mundane.

Some additional low stress marketing activities to work in around your "too busy to market" schedule include:

- sending a thank-you card to a referral source

- inviting a prospect out to a mutually interesting business event

- listening to what your clients and contacts are complaining about – there may be gold there

- calling people on their birthdays

- scanning a trade magazine or the internet to pick up a sense of timely issues before seeing a client or prospect in that industry

Over the years, it turned out that many of the professionals who swore to me that they were the "exception" – that they "really were too busy," simply detested business development and preferred to do other things.

It's probably more about how you approach marketing and what you actually do, than the tasks themselves that cause angst.

It really is your mindset that rules.

<End of sample>

How to Make Your Firm a Better Place Than You Found It by Walter Timoshenko is scheduled for release in 2015.

An excerpt from the book

**OFFICIAL BUSINESS DEVELOPMENT SERIES
for Professionals**
Networking Success

Teamwork & the Power of the Third Party Endorsement

Ever go to an event only to meet someone who is very impressed with … themselves?

They go on and on about how great they are. *Yawn.* And just when you think they are finished, they turn to you and say, "Oh, enough about me talking about me. Let's find out what you think about me."

Painful.

But here is the conundrum.

You want to say great stuff about yourself to catch the attention of prospective clients. You want to throw in all those things you know you are so great at.

But then you worry that if you boast about yourself, then you will sound, well, like a complete jerk. So, do you get overly modest and downplay stuff? Not very effective.

What to do?

Over the course of many years of trial and error, I discovered a very effective strategy to overcome this hurdle. One word.

Teamwork. Team up with someone so both of you can then "work" the room together.

Here is how it works. You and I team up and attend a networking event with one another. We walk the room and approach people as a team and speak to them together.

One hand washes the other

In a very brief and conversational manner, I introduce you as a consummate professional, mention your top areas of expertise, your main service offerings, and end with several very successful outcomes you've had for thrilled clients. I then turn it over to you as I say something along the lines of, "Well, I think I got that right but is there anything I missed?" You thank me and proceed to add a little more color as you build your brand image. Then we turn to the other person and ask them about themselves. Once they are done, you turn to me and introduce me as I just did for you.

Once the intros are over, and during the regular conversation, we continue to help each other. For instance, after you mention a new service you are offering, I can chime in and add something relevant, such as how that service benefitted someone I know, et cetera. Then you make a comment that leads into what I do and after I tell a short story about what I do and how it has helped a client, you jump in and vouch for me and my services.

Water ballet

Great care must be taken not to sound rehearsed or to fawn. Keep it real and natural. Stay true and honest. Yet don't forget to sell me a little as I will sell you. It takes practice, but when it works, it's like water ballet.

You cannot imagine how highly effective this approach can be, especially when you are virtually unknown to the prospective client or referral source.

<End of sample>

(*Networking Success* by Walter Timoshenko, in a newly updated edition, is currently available on Amazon in both print and electronic versions.)

Special acknowledgements

Over the years I have been blessed to have worked with and around great minds and talents. Some I knew for years, others for mere moments. Yet they all made lasting impressions. If we could only be so lucky to have more of them in circulation.

In *NO* particular order, my sincerest thanks to the following individuals for everything they've taught me:

Isaac Asimov, Brian Tracy, Bill Martin, Marcia Golden, Gavin McElroy, Stephen Black, Marty Garbus, Mike Xirinachs, Brian Murphy, Malcolm Petrook, LN Crone, Bean're (again), Jeff Greenbaum, Morty Weber, John Irving, Charlie Flood, Harold Levine, Ed Vick, Henry Ruhnke, Barbara Berger Opotowsky, Jim Galowski, Original Hammer, Rebel– RIP, Bill Hammer, Emilio Estevez, Vinny Sullivan, Al Pacino, Tom Selz, Andy Muscolino, Big Mike, Copper Mike, Jim Garner, and Matthew Lynford Shafer.

And to the countless others I have no doubt overlooked unintentionally – a million thanks to you, too!

About the author

Walter Timoshenko provides brand management, marketing, and communications guidance and training for professional services firms, businesses, corporations, and NFPs. He specializes in assisting Partners, Managing Members, MPs, Executive Committees, CEOs, Niche Leaders, and other executives at professional services firms to align their marketing, management, and communications strategies for success.

Named by Accounting Today as one of the "Top 100 Most Influential People," Walter created and served as the first Chairman of the AICPA's *Accounting Firm Marketing Forum* held annually in New York City. He also delivers speeches and presentations on marketing, branding, and communications across the country, and was featured at the AICPA's *Future of Accounting Leadership Forum.*

As an associate member of the American Bar Association, Walter helped launch one of the earliest series for legal marketing seminars, and frequently taught CLE related courses at the Association of the Bar of the City of New York, as well as at various law schools.

A regular contributor to the professional services marketing and branding site www.TotalBrandMarketing.com, Walter wrote the foreword for "The 7 Secrets of Extraordinary Investors" by Grammy-Award winner William G. Hammer, Jr., and edited a variety of technical books on financing and legal defense. A long-time member of Mensa and *Beta Gamma Sigma*, he was named the first *Henry O. Ruhnke Executive of the Year* for his dedication to the *Executive in Residence Program* at the Tobin College of Business.

A personal thank you to you!
And a favor…

Thank you for taking your time to purchase and read this *Presentation Success* guide! I hope that it serves you well and helps you get more success out of your business development activities.

If you feel that this guide has helped you, I would be sincerely grateful if you would post a short review on Amazon and recommend this guide to others who would benefit as well.

Clearly a broad topic such as making successful presentations with its limitless situational variables can't be fully covered in a book. My consulting and training practice provides that *extra mile*, tailored to your situation. If you are interested in taking your practice or your firm to that *next level,* please feel free to reach out to me.

In the meanwhile, if you have any questions, comments, suggestions, or ideas about this guide, please email me at WT@TotalBrandMarketing.com

Thanks again and have a terrific day!

How would you like to learn, in less than 10 minutes, how to instantly increase the power of just one of your marketing ideas up to 12 times by harnessing the power of *"Power Spin-Offs!"*?

Since this free report offer may be withdrawn
or modified at any time,
go NOW to

www.TotalBrandMarketing.com

to subscribe to our FREE newsletter and claim your FREE report.

23067076R00044

Made in the USA
Middletown, DE
15 August 2015